10 Ways To Make Sure You Never Stop Being Defensive

by C Kruse

Table of Contents

PROLOGUE.

Defensiveness. What is it, other than a four syllable word? What images does the word give you? The root word, defense, means "to resist an attack" or to "protect from harm or danger." The word "defend" might make you think of an ancient city's fortitudes, built to keep its inhabitants safe. The Great Wall of China may come to mind – that thirteen thousand mile wonder, put up to protect China from raids and invasions along its western border.

In sports, we often hear that the best offense is a good defense. Winning a game isn't just about how many goals your team can score, but just as much about minimizing how many goals the other team scores. The best way to be a good, effective team, is to have a strong defense.

We also commonly hear the word "defense" used in the context of self-defense, which is what a person does (or attempts to do) when he/she is threatened and, rather than lying down or retreating, fights back.

In most examples where we see the word "defense" being used, it has positive connotations. By this, we might easily assume that defensiveness is a good quality. But actually, in most cases that involve human relationships, defensiveness has more negative than positive value.

Take for example; romantic relationships. John Gottman, relationships expert and author of "The Relationship Cure," refers to defensiveness as one of the four "horsemen of the relational apocalypse." In other words, when you see it coming, look out... the end is near!

Miriam Webster's Dictionary defines defensiveness as: behaving in a way that shows that you feel people are criticizing you. Author Shannon L. Alder says that "Defensiveness is usually someone silently screaming that they need you to value and respect them..."

But perhaps we know defensiveness best by its common outward manifestations - the ways a person will constantly make excuses, deflect criticisms, needlessly disagree or insist on being right. Sometimes it's what we witness in other people. Sometimes we see it in ourselves, coming out in the "It's not my fault" remarks, or the "Yeah, but you" retorts.

But we aren't always aware that this behavior reveals something about us… that deep down, we feel we have something to prove. Which only means that despite how confident or courageous we want to appear, somewhere inside, we feel inadequate or unworthy. We believe our value is contingent upon others' affirmations.

These feelings are often deeply ingrained into us. Some of them, stemming back to experiences from our childhoods, which over the years have woven their effects into our dispositions. For that reason, it has become incredibly hard for us to recognize our own defensiveness or to know how to change it.

To make matters worse, we often detach from our rational minds when we become defensive. Emotions run high, and it becomes nearly impossible for us to "let down our guards." This makes defensiveness into a matter that is not just psychological or emotional, but also, physical. Maybe this explains why defensiveness is so hard to overcome.

Judge Jim Tamm, former law professional, says that "remaining non-defensive is the single most important thing you can do to increase your effectiveness when working to turn conflict into collaboration." What can we say so far about overcoming defensiveness? That not only is it one of the hardest things we could ever do, it's also one of the most crucial.

But what makes defensiveness such a hard problem to solve is its propensity to stay hidden. It's a problem that we trace back to everyone but ourselves. It's your spouse's fault that you don't trust people. It's your family's fault that you can't take a joke.

These people who've provoked us in some way, we believe, are the ones who have problems. Therefore, why should we be the ones reading a self-help book, delving deep into our psyches? Let's save that hard work for the people who need it.

But the thing is, defensiveness *is* our problem. It doesn't matter who provokes us… whether it's our neighbor, our spouse or a tree falling in the woods, it only hurts us when we respond negatively to such things.

And, if a real solution exists out there, it's not something we can force on anyone else. It must begin in ourselves, as we are the only ones we have power to change. As author Stephen Covey said, "Our ultimate freedom is the right and power to decide how anybody or anything outside ourselves will affect us."

We need to overcome defensiveness, perhaps most of all, because criticism is everywhere. Even when we do a job 99% right, it seems someone is still only going to notice the 1% we missed. And if our reasons stemmed from a need to feel appreciated, we will almost certainly react poorly when confronted or quit a job before it is finished.

There is simply no escaping criticism. If you look at all relationships, you'll find that it exists in even the healthiest of them. Good friends must sometimes say "Hey Steve, you parked your car in my spot again," or "Bob, why didn't you tell anyone you drank the last of the milk?" Even the most loving spouses must sometimes say, "Hey, you're stealing the covers," or "You forgot to put the toothpaste cap back on."

But a person's defensiveness might make him unable to hear even such small things without rising up in defense. He sees them as an attack, when quite often, they aren't. In fact, they're often even acts of love. As the old proverb says, better are the wounds of a friend than the kisses of an enemy.

If we aren't able to hear criticism well, even when delivered lovingly, then the problem isn't on the end of the sender, but on the end of the receiver. If we get defensive, there is no way around it… we are the ones doing damage to our relationships.

To see if you fall into the "defensive" category, I've developed a small quiz. Please answer the following ten questions.

1. Do you take it personally when someone criticizes you?
2. Do you feel a greater sense of personal worth when somebody compliments you?

3. Do you often feel like you are in competition with those you talk to?

4. Do you have a hard time letting others acknowledge your imperfections?

5. Do you commonly view people as "offensive?"

6. Do you get worked up when people rub you the wrong way?

7. Are you sometimes too distracted by a person's words and body language to hear the message in what he's saying?

8. Are you normally suspicious of people's true, hidden motives?

9. Do you blame other people for your own reactions?

10. Do you commonly feel undervalued?

Take a look at your results. If you answered "yes" to three or more of these questions, you are probably a more defensive person. And if you respond negatively to hearing that you're a defensive person, then the chances are even greater that yes, you indeed are a defensive person.

They always say the first step toward recovery is admitting that you have a problem. So, if you are a defensive person, then I want you to pause for a moment and say it out loud. Say; "I have a problem with defensiveness. With this problem, I am doing great harm to my relationships." From there, you can begin to move forward and make real changes.

Defensiveness robs us of a better life. It keeps us from having better positions at work, better relationships at home, better friendships, better communication, and even, the chance to be made better by valuable constructive criticism. Isn't it time we stop doing this?

Welcome to 10 ways to make sure you never stop being defensive. In this book, we will tell you all about the ten rules to follow if your goal is to stay defensive forever. These rules, of course, are rules that you should break, being that your goal probably is not to stay defensive forever, but to improve and experience a healthier world.

The ten rules are:

1. Personalize Matters That Aren't Personal.
2. Make All Matters Into Matters Of Worthiness.
3. Look For Offenses In Everything.
4. Assume To Know What Others Are Thinking.
5. Dodge The Blame.
6. Always Speak And Act Before Thinking.
7. Do Not Be Self-Aware.

8.   Do Not Hear The Message Behind The Words.
9.   Always Be Right.
10. Never Take Any Crap From Anyone.

So, without further ado, let's begin with:

RULE # 1.
PERSONALIZE
MATTERS THAT AREN'T
PERSONAL.

It's a common expression in business, when a deal is unfavorable, for one party to say to the other "it's not personal, just business." It's also common outside of business for people to say "Don't take it personally." It's the follow-up phrase we hear when we're the last ones picked by the team captains, when our coworkers get promoted over us, or when we're told by our dates that we're really, really nice, but unfortunately, not what they're looking for. Ouch.

The strange thing is that almost anytime you and I are on the receiving end of criticism or rejection, we find it very hard not to take it personally. In fact, we have a hard time seeing how it can be *anything but* personal. Maybe a better understanding is what we need.

First of all, what does the phrase "it's not personal" mean? Literally, it could probably be translated to: "it's not about the person." So, if you and I are rejected, it's not about us as people. It's usually about other things, like the requirements of a position that we do or don't meet, the basketball skills that we do or don't possess, or the attributes that a potential lover wants which we do or don't have. We may feel personally rejected, but the rejection is no more pertinent to us than it is to anybody else.

Think about the rule that a speed limit sign enforces. It applies to everyone on the road - not just to you, but also, to the driver behind you, as well as to the driver approaching in the oncoming lane. The speed limit sign is indifferent. It doesn't like you more if you obey it. Nor does it like you less if you disobey it. It only states a rule… one that you can either choose to acknowledge, or choose to see as a personal attack aimed specifically at you.

In this way, defensiveness is often rooted in a self-centered focus, where a person cannot see anything more to a matter than how it pertains to him. If the person at the drive through line is rude to him, he takes it personally. If a cop writes him a ticket, he takes it personally. If someone tells him he's not qualified enough for a job position, he takes it personally.

Some mental health disorders, like paranoia, are characterized by a type of self-aggrandizing that is similar (yet more severe), in which a person feels confident that the world is "out to get him." He thinks that hidden cameras are all around him. He believes big brother is listening in on his conversations. In his imaginary world, he is so important that he can't fathom being anywhere but at the center of all that happens to him. This is what we're doing as well when we take impersonal matters personally.

Most things that we perceive as personal attacks, usually aren't. The guy at the drive through line who was rude to you doesn't even know you. Nor did the cop who wrote you a ticket. Nor did the employer who said you weren't qualified for the job. If you see them as personal attacks, you're more than likely jumping to bad conclusions.

And, you're almost guaranteed not to see the real reasons behind your loved ones' behavior. Maybe that friend who snapped at you has been feeling overwhelmed. And maybe your brother, who hasn't been returning your calls, has been feeling like a failure ever since his kids have been ignoring him. All these people, you could be helping, if you weren't too busy feeling hurt. Choosing not to be defensive will open up key opportunities to show love in people's lives.

Sometimes it's hard not to take things personally… especially in closer relationships, which involve higher levels of trust and expectation. It's one thing to feel offended by a stranger. It's a whole other thing to feel offended by someone you know and trust and expect a great deal more from. As the saying goes, "we always hurt the ones we love." The ones we love, it seems, are the ones we have greater capacity to wound. It would do us well to learn not to have such a "strong defense." In fact, relationships seem to flourish far more when we lower our walls, rather than raise them.

We could learn a lot about overcoming defensiveness by observing the masters - people like Hellen Keller, who was born with physical limitations, subjecting her to a lifetime of being judged and misunderstood. Or, Victor Frankl, who learned not to let his soul become bitter and tainted by the cruelty of a Nazi concentration camp.

These people seemed to realize that others' unkindnesses were almost like a contagious sickness… one that they themselves didn't want to catch. You and I could realize the same… that when someone is bitter towards us and we let ourselves become bitter by it, we've become infected by the disease they exposed us to. How can we form an immunity to the sicknesses floating around out there?

The healthiest solution you and I could learn to apply is to practice loving people. Even if you're unsure whether or not they have good intentions. Even if you know their intentions are bad. Don't catch their sickness. Worry about being well yourself, and possibly, infecting them with the positivity, charisma and affection that you've learned to carry instead.

Recap:

To make sure that you stay defensive forever, this is what you should do. Next time you see or hear something that offends you, whether it's a look, a tone or a tree falling in the woods, make it all about you. Take it personally. Don't separate yourself from what is happening. Try to realize that other people's rude smirks, aggressive statements, unthoughtful comments and actions, are reflections of who you are as a person. Don't allow anything to happen without it becoming a personal matter.

RULE # 2. MAKE ALL MATTERS INTO MATTERS OF WORTHINESS.

One thing about we humans is that so many of us are trying to find worth outside of ourselves. We're trying to be loved for how attractive we are, how much money we make or how many credentials we've collected. We get our senses of worth, not by uncovering our intrinsic value, but by acquiring superficial traits that we think others will admire.

I noticed when I was younger that I felt more appreciated when I was helpful. And, when I got good grades in school. Doing praiseworthy things actually seemed to make me worthy of other people's praise. And, worthy of their affection.

This seemed to settle somewhere deep in my thinking, affecting the choices I made academically, relationally and career wise. It became the hidden motivator, steering me into directions that others wanted me to go in. And most of the time, it gave me a great sense of accomplishment. Especially when I was right on track. But as soon as the good performance stopped, so did the affirmations. It felt like my value could suddenly plummet to zero.

I began to notice that this system of finding worth was a large part of why I was so defensive. Anytime someone told me I was doing poorly, it felt like they were criticizing more than my performance... more like they were really criticizing me as a person, attacking my self-worth.

This is how we can make any matter into a matter of worthiness. It's why we resent being criticized, and why we take to heart everything that's said of us at performance reviews. The truth we've somehow lost sight of is that such things aren't connected to our value in any way.   Of course, there will be those who base our value on our performance, but they're not the ones whose opinions we should care about anyway.

Not long ago I was talking with my life-coach. He asked me to explain what I like about myself. The question caught me by surprise. I couldn't even think of a few things to say. When after a few minutes I was still just as speechless, he decided to make it my assignment for the next two weeks.

As time went by I tried to give it some thought, occasionally coming up with things like "Well, sometimes I'm pretty nice," or "I'm good at being creative," but all the reasons I came up with felt like fluff, as though I was only making them up to make myself feel better.

To make a long story short, it took me a good deal of searching to actually find traits about myself that I liked and that I actually believed. What I learned is that this key thing -

knowing your worth is not an easy task. And yet, it is an extremely essential part of the quest to become less defensive.

Staying grounded in this area is paramount, and it's a constant struggle for many. Most of us who aren't in touch with our self-worth would rather not delve into searching for it. We're afraid there's nothing to find, or like me, we don't think the good truths are as genuine or as defining as the negative truths. But until we know where our self-worth lies, we will always be extremely susceptible to becoming defensive.

Once you've found it, you won't be nearly as prone to making things into matters of worthiness. How do you find it? Well, to start, let's look at where it isn't; it's not in your car. It's not in your skills or your accomplishments. It's not in your title or your paycheck. It is only in one place... inside of you. And if you learn to become sure of where it is, then nothing will ever be able to make you wonder if it's there.

Recap:

So, to make sure you never stop being defensive, just make sure that you make all matters into matters of worthiness. See criticisms as assessments of your value, having to do with who you are as a person.

RULE # 3. LOOK FOR OFFENSES IN EVERYTHING.

When we are defensive, it is because we perceive some threat that we must protect ourselves from. Whether or not that is actual is almost beside the point. Because as soon as we think there is one, we become defensive, and our body language begins to show it.

It has been called a "defensive posture" when a person folds his arms and crosses his legs upon feeling shy or socially awkward. This, because subconsciously, he is protecting himself from any unknown, perceived, or potential threats.

But more interesting is how such posturing is received by others. When we walk into a situation with suspicion or with the perception that there is a threat, it only causes others to notice that we sense a threat, and to look for it as well. Defensive posturing may only cause others to reciprocate with defensive posturing of their own. Funny how we can actually encourage defensiveness in others simply by exuding it ourselves.

In defensive interactions, valuable time is wasted trying to establish good intentions. Generally, people don't like giving the courtesy of trust if they don't feel it is mutual. To some degree, healthy interactions require that we give the benefit of the doubt. Why? Because doubt is in everything. Think of all the variables in life that are simply beyond our knowing.

Your friend says he'll call you later, but for some reason, doesn't. What do you do? You can either assume that he has good reasons, or you can assume you were wrong about his character, and that he is a liar. Either way, you must assume something. What you assume will directly affect the friendship.

So many outcomes depend on our tendencies to either believe the worst or believe the best. And such tendencies depend on our posturing, or our chosen dispositions to all that we encounter. The heart is a bit like a hand. When it is closed, it makes a fist, which is good for protecting, but bad at accepting gifts. An open hand however, can accept gifts, but it is less inclined to defend itself. Similarly, by choosing our posture, we are also choosing whether or not we want to reject or receive love.

It is common for those of us who've been injured to build up walls of protection around our hearts, and to choose that posture that is similar to a closed fist. There is a problem with this. Not so much that it is ineffective at keeping threats out, but that it is almost too effective. It keeps out all things… bad and good alike.

The problem is that love and hurt travel together. You cannot allow one while restricting the other, or restrict one while allowing the other. The closed-fist posture of defensiveness restricts both, rather than allows both. Funny that of all the threats that we create a wall to avoid, the greatest threat to our joy is usually the wall itself.

Of course there have been times in our lives when a wall has been needed. People have wanted to do us harm, and we've needed a form of protection. But the problem with a wall comes later on, when we continue to keep it up long after it has served its purpose. A soldier's armor is only good for him in battle. When he comes home and eats, sleeps and spends time with his family, it would only be a hindrance to him if he kept on wearing it.

Sometimes we may not know if our armor is still necessary, as life is full of uncertainties. Sometimes it's hard to tell if the people around do or don't have good character (and good intentions). Are there any rules of thumb that we can generally go by? Yes. It would do us good to realize that all humans have both good and bad in them. Whichever we find usually depends on which we are looking for.

Defensiveness is the search that starts out looking for the negative. And since we usually find what we're looking for, our defensiveness leads us to find all the threats and bad traits in people that we were anticipating.

Recap:

So, do not be open about your insecurities. Nor should you ever let others think that you trust them. This shows weakness. Don't let them offer to help you either. Trust your suspicions of them and don't consider more positive alternatives. Do not retrain your brain. Allow your suspicions to mature into beliefs.

RULE # 4. ASSUME TO KNOW WHAT OTHERS ARE THINKING.

Not long ago, I had an important phone call to make. I needed to speak to person in a position of power for permission in order to begin a certain project I was working on - one that I was very involved in. I was nervous before calling, because I knew that a lot depended on how our conversation would go.

When he answered the phone, we exchanged greetings. I fumbled to get to my point, even admitting that I was a bit nervous. He told me I shouldn't be, and seemed very polite. After a few minutes, I felt like I had finally expressed myself. He said he needed to think about my request a little bit before getting back to me.

When we hung up, I still felt nervous. I wasn't sure how our conversation had gone. I waited to hear back from him, but my phone wasn't ringing. One week went by. Then, another. Then, another yet. A whole month had gone by. Soon, I was counting the days after a month. My anxiety was starting to consume me.

I didn't know why he wasn't calling, and started to form some assumptions. I thought, "maybe he just doesn't like me," or, "maybe he thinks I don't deserve this." This made me wonder if I was a likable person, or if there was some flaw in me that others noticed that I should try to change. Though my rejection was imaginary, it started to feel very real. So real, that I was beginning to strategize defenses.

I eventually picked up the phone and called, knowing that whatever he had to say couldn't have been worse than what I had been imagining.

I sat there listening to the ringing sound, waiting for that grumpy, condescending person to answer. But instead, I heard a very polite, pleasant voice say "hello?" What was this? Had I dialed the wrong number? He actually sounded happy to hear from me when he remembered who I was, and he apologized for having not gotten back to me in so long. He had been swamped with work and under abnormal circumstances. Within minutes, I had the permission I needed, and the peace of mind that all my assuming had taken. Needless to say, the phone call was worth it.

But I began to see how my mind has a way of running amuck when it is uncertain - that I, rather than give someone the benefit of the doubt, will sometimes rely upon negative assumptions that my mind conjures up.

At times you're left with no choice but to make an assumption. You're left waiting, like me, and you simply don't know what type of outcome to expect. The problem seems to arise when our assumptions become negative. We end up fearing and planning for a crisis that often doesn't ever materialize. Then, dealing with the stress of the imaginary crisis we created.

There is no reward in this type of thinking. Not only do you waste precious sleep, time and energy... not only do you deprive yourself of anticipating positive outcomes that are just as (or even more) probable, you also end up putting yourself in a position to be defensive, and to do harm to a relationship. After all, if you assume people think ill of you, you're more likely to be on the defense against them.

Because I learned something important here... in that time, while I was waiting for the telephone to ring. I saw how I was actually starting to defend myself in advance from the imaginary attacks I foresaw. I was gloving up to defend myself against someone who only wished me well... someone who really, was a very kind, gentle person. When you assume you know somebody's motives, you might never actually learn what their true motives are. And in this case, look how mislead I would have been if I had settled to trust my assumptions. I wonder... how often is our defensiveness like this? Not based on anything substantial, but on pure misguided (and emotionally skewed) assumptions?

In all of this, I've also realized how our own histories play an important role in how we perceive. Generally, our past hurts can make it very hard for us to give people the benefit of the doubt. Our negative assumptions about people usually stem from feelings of shame or rejection we've felt in the past. We link present moments to the past, even though they may not be nothing like the past events we remember. In this way, our perspectives of reality have little to do with what's actually real. More to do with what we feel.

And, because of this, the quest to become less defensive (and truly more free overall), is largely about learning to let past hurts go. This is not easy. In fact, it will be a long, strenuous journey, filled with proactive intention. Old views are hardwired into us - they are the safety nets our hearts look to fall on when threatened. The walls we find shelter behind from imaginary rejections.

Make it a goal of yours to discover and re-write your prejudices, and to realize beforehand that the process of doing this will not feel natural at all. You will be stepping outside your comfort zone. This important step will strengthen not just you, but your relationships with everyone you know… a step that will no doubt be worth it in the long run.

Recap:

To ensure that you stay defensive forever, be certain to nurture your prejudices. Keep on feeding the misconceptions about other that you've formed about them being threats to your self-worth, and having intentions to do you harm. Keep expecting them to be offensive, and you'll be well on your way to creating the expectations you anticipate.

RULE # 5. DODGE THE BLAME.

Let's look now at one very indisputable fact about humans - we all have flaws. Those of us who claim to be more enlightened will even say that we aware of our flaws. Yet many of us, despite how enlightened we are, still seem to spend an awful lot of time burying our flaws, denying they're there... even feeling attacked whenever other people acknowledge them. So, the question for us is this: If our flaws really are as obvious as we say, then why do we have such a hard time noticing, being shown or dealing with the obvious?

The simple truth is, many of us are trying to deal with our flaws, not by facing them, but by pretending they're not there, wishfully hoping we've overcome them and diverting others' attention away from them whenever we sense they are starting to notice. This defense mechanism, called deflection, is sometimes accomplished with the use of humor. Or, a person may simply attempt to change the subject. A lot of us have become crafty, like lawyers or politicians, drawing attention away from facts that don't favor us, while drawing attention towards the ones that do.

But the most damaging type of deflection happens when we, upon feeling criticized, attack the person that criticizes us. We may try to discredit or invalidate them. We may try to use the exact same criticism on them that they used on us. We look for a fault in them to point out, to serve as proof that they have no right to judge us. The purpose of this is usually that a person feels insecure in himself, and his sense of self-satisfaction depends on being perceived well.

Deflection stems from an "either-or" way of thinking, in which one believes that only one party can be at fault. He thinks; "either them... or me." To keep himself from being the guilty party, he must make sure that the guilt is somebody else's. And usually, who better to blame than the one doing the accusing? So, he deflects, and kills two birds with one stone - He assigns guilt to someone else while absolving himself of having any.

Deflective people usually feel that their wrongdoings are justified because of the wrongdoings of others. They rationalize their aggression by whatever they feel provoked by. This is very damaging in relationships, where defensiveness works to undermine the logic and feelings of others. Your spouse tells you that you left dishes in the sink. Rather than admit it and say you're sorry, you remind her of the dishes she accidentally broke last week. What does this prove? Two things; one, that you aren't really interested in knowing her thoughts or feelings. And two, that you're willing to risk injuring her in order to avoid being wrong.

If relationships truly do depend on love and trust and openness, then it's no wonder why defensive deflection is such a relationship killer. And yet, how many of us habitually do this

to the ones we love most? A shockingly sad, large amount.
Let's learn not to be deflectors of criticism.

The best thing we can do is learn to admit our faults. Stop
ourselves when we sense that we are starting to deflect. If we
let others know we're starting to feel defensive, it might allow
them to tailor their dealings with us in a careful, helpful way.

Admitting that you are defensive can be a disarming thing,
both for you and whoever you are speaking to. And, if you're
open about your weaknesses, you invite others to help you
with them. This can actually be something that strengthens
your relationships, rather than harms them.

Recap:

So, here is what you can walk away with: deflect all criticisms
and complaints away from yourself and back toward the
sender. See your defensiveness as somebody else's problem,
rather than your own. Why should you be responsible for how

you react? Always stew on your hurts, and remember - your self-worth depends on how blameless you can appear.

RULE # 6. ALWAYS SPEAK AND ACT BEFORE THINKING.

As a boy in school, I loved to write. My favorite assignments involved essays, where I could express myself in great depth. I did them quite naturally. Yet even so, I always found that no matter how good I thought they were, they still needed editing. Sometimes I'd have to rewrite entire pages and scratch sections out before they finally expressed what I wanted to say.

Now, as an adult, I realize how much this has taught me about life. Quite often, my impulses are like the rough drafts I used to write… they flow naturally, but they aren't the truest expressions of what I want to say. They need quite a bit of "editing" before they are reflecting my truest thoughts and feelings. Whenever I act or speak upon these "rough-draft" urges, I almost always say what doesn't represent me. And, I almost always regret it.

Many of us can think of numerous occasions when we've done or said things we've wished we could take back. In our modern technological age, it may even harder for us to "take back" our actions or words, due to the fact that everyone now has cameras and recorders on their digital devices. How many of us have seen how unintelligent our defensiveness has made us look on film or in pictures?

Why? Because defensiveness actually does make us less intelligent. At least, temporarily. No matter how sane or rational we are in our clear moments, we can become like impulsive animals during the heat of our battles. During these moments, our "fight or flight" responses can be triggered, causing our pulses and respiratory rates to increase. And, causing our blood flow to divert away from our cores to our extremities, decreasing our abilities to think rationally. Our IQs actually drop, making us less intelligent. And as though that weren't enough, we seem to also momentarily stop caring about consequences.

These changes make us all capable of living split lives, like Doctor Jekyll and Mr. Hyde. Our irrational sides are always getting us into deep trouble, while our more rational sides are always bailing us out. It would be in our best interests to learn how to stop ourselves from acting in our defensiveness before we get too far.

For many of us, this is the one thing keeping us from having the relationships we dream of - the inability to keep our mouths shut while we're irrational. If we could simply learn how to withhold our thoughts until we cool down, we'd thank ourselves later for the relationships, time and credibility that we spared.

So often we can't even remember what our arguments were about. How important can something be if it's not even worth remembering later? Certainly not more than the peace and harmony we were temporarily willing to trade it for.

Also, we should realize that few problems are ever really solved in the heat of the moment. Rarely is this the time when good decisions are made, or when big decisions should be contemplated. The effect of winning an argument is that somebody else loses. That person may have conceded, but at heart, he has probably only become more determined to rise up and get you back later on.

Let's put this play in our playbooks; to peacefully, politely disengage from a conflict until our heads are cool. That way, we'll have fewer holes to dig ourselves out of.

Recap:

So, the important thing to remember is this; when you sense defensive behavior overcoming you, be sure to do and say whatever feels right. Do not self-soothe. Do not mentally detach from the situation or attempt to come back to your senses. It's too late. Follow your emotions, because they are in control. Do whatever you must in order to make your points loud and clear. Win the argument, even if it means jeopardizing your relationships and your credibility.

RULE # 7. DO NOT BE SELF-AWARE.

In the classic comedy, What About Bob, there is a funny scene in which Bob, a chronically anxious patient played by Bill Murray, takes a bus to New Hampshire to find Dr. Marvin, a psychiatrist played by Richard Dreyfus, on vacation.

When Bob arrives in New Hampshire, he manages to find Dr. Marvin by pure chance at a local store. Dr. Marvin is shocked and frustrated upon seeing him. Bob senses that he is upset and says "you're angry."

Dr. Marvin expresses in a somewhat defensive way, "I don't get angry."

"You're upset."

"I don't get upset."

I've always found this scene humorous for a number of reasons. Mostly because this psychiatrist who is supposed to be trained in human behavior, isn't sharp enough to see or admit when he is beginning to feel worked up and defensive.

But I've realized how we all are a bit like this... somewhat blind to the obvious emotional changes happening in us. Others often see these things in us before we do. Sometimes, like in this situation, they try to tell us that we're becoming worked up. We may deny it defensively. How can we be so unaware? It seems to be because the changes in us happen gradually.

We've all heard the metaphor of the frog that sits in water until it slowly reaches a boil. In a way, this describes how we can be in our defensiveness. By the time our heated emotions become apparent to us, they have already been evolving for some time. Our first indication that we're worked up is when we find ourselves wanting to punch a hole in the wall.

A large part of that battle for us is to simply learn what it is that triggers our defensiveness, and to notice when it has been triggered. This will drastically reduce our chances of doing damage to our relationships in the heat of the moment.

Maybe you start to become defensive when you feel you aren't being listened to. Maybe it's when you feel disrespected. Maybe it's when somebody around you, either at work or at home, treats you in such a way that reminds you of a poor way you used to be treated a long time ago, even though there may be no threat present.

And, once your defensiveness has been triggered, there may be certain ways you start to respond. You may become short and snippy. You might respond sarcastically. Perhaps you form a nervous twitch or you shuffle your feet anxiously. Whatever it is, it's good to notice what is happening as soon as possible, because this is the sign that your proverbial pot of water is reaching a boil.

It would be a very good practice for you to write down your list of defensive reactions and keep that list handy so that you train yourself to start looking for those reactions in your day-to-day life. And if you really want to make some large strides, then here's an even more daring Idea that I recommend: ask some people who know you well to tell you how you act when you become defensive. Allowing them to have this type of input and influence will serve two purposes. 1. It will help you overcome your resistance to hearing criticism from others, and 2. It will provide you with some valuable information about yourself.

The next step is; learning what to do with that valuable information. Notice those defensive reactions when they start happening, and form a plan of action. This would be a good time to practice some self-soothing techniques, to help bring you to an overall state of calmness and being less likely to act out of defensiveness.

Turn on your favorite classical album and listen to it through headphones. Take a five minute break to meditate and focus on your breathing. Do some physical exercises that give you a healthy distraction and help you re-center your mind on a positive focus. Taking these small intentional actions during crucial moments can have the most amazing, noticeable results.

Recap:

So, in your goal to make sure you never stop being defensive, it is good to remember that you should not be self-aware. Do not notice when the temperature of emotional waters are changing. Tune out those pesky thoughts about heeding the danger. They interfere with your lighthearted state of denial. No matter what you do, do not attempt to deescalate the situation.

RULE # 8. DO NOT HEAR THE MESSAGE BEHIND THE WORDS.

One problem when we're defensive is the shift that happens in our goals. We become less interested in hearing what a person has to say, more interested in the way they are saying it… their tones, body language or word choice. We become so wrapped up in these things that we fail to notice the most important thing - the message they're conveying.

We would probably all agree that the main point of communicating isn't just to make noise, but to share thoughts, feelings and ideas… to exchange information and to have dialogue. And, that if communicating ever becomes about something besides this, that its purpose has been lost.

Here, we have another way in which defensiveness does us harm. When we lose the value of communication, we lose the tool that could make our lives better. We even seem to temporarily stop caring about what could make our lives better. In these moments, we are in desperate need of becoming re-centered in our focuses. This will help us to remember the real goals in communicating, lest we become sidetracked.

We can put our focuses back onto what matters. Of course, this is something we must learn to do before things escalate, rather than in the heat of the moment. If we wait until we're hot and raging, this solution probably won't be of as much help.

Here's how it can work. Start off by making a list of the things that matter to you. To find them, you may have to set some time aside to do a little soul-searching. On your next day off, try to see the big picture. Think about what kind of legacy you'd like to leave behind when you die. What words would you like others to say of you in your eulogy? What would you like to have written on your tombstone?

As you find the answers to these questions, write them down. You'll slowly start to come back in touch with truths that are more important than the silly battles you sometimes feel obsessed with winning. This can be something that gives you strength during crucial moments to see the message behind the words, rather than the words themselves or how they're delivered.

The next time you hear your coworker crabbing, saying "nobody ever does their job around here," you will be better suited to look past her tones and her grumpy facial expressions, and to hear the actual message she is trying to convey. That is; "Help. Please! I need somebody to notice my needs."   And then, upon hearing her true message, you can run to a telephone booth and put your cape on. You can swoop in and start solving problems, rather than adding to them by reciprocating with accusations.

You might even find the strangest need arising in you to apologize for times in the past when you have been uncaring or unobservant… crimes you weren't able to see your part in back when you were too busy trying to defend yourself. Or, you may feel that her criticism is mostly untrue regarding you. But either way, you aren't taking it personally. You're doing something far more important. You're hearing the message behind her words.

Recap:

Remember - you must never pause and re-center your focus on what matters. Do not be concerned with results, and pay lots of attention to others' word choice, tone usage and body language. This matters far more than the message they're trying to convey.

RULE # 9. ALWAYS BE RIGHT.

For defensive people, it is usually very important to be right. And, they feel that in order to be right, somebody else must be wrong. Their either/or mentalities keep them focused on only one side of a matter, and from seeing other sides that may be just as true. This tendency causes them to get into more disagreements.

A person may be talking about the state of Washington, saying that it is unique for its topography. But a defensive person, upon hearing this, might feel the need to disagree, saying that Washington is unique, not for its topography, but for its rainy climate. The defensive person doesn't realize that they can both be right, and that their statements don't contradict each other. Because of this, he works unnecessarily to negate his opponent's statement.

We see here how there are even more ways in which defensiveness can be harmful in relationships, as it usually puts our focus on winning, holding on tightly to something we did right, even if the sum total of our actions were mostly wrong.

A man who gets cited for speeding might argue that he normally never speeds. He might say he wasn't speeding *that* much, or that his intentions weren't *that* bad. He might justify his speeding by talking about circumstances that caused him to be in a hurry. He might claim to be related to the guy who invented the speed limit sign. But, of all the things he does and says, he fails to do the one thing that would probably make the biggest difference - admit his error and apologize for it.

And this is how you and I are as well. During those moments when we are in the wrong, rather than admit we are wrong, we search for any aspect of the case in which we are right, and we cling to it like it's the last life raft on the Titanic. But the more determined we are not to see our faults, it seems the more resolute others are to bring them to our attention. Dale Carnegie once said, "Apologize for your mistakes. It will help disarm your opponents and reduce defensiveness."

There's something about those simple words, "I'm sorry," that are so diffusing. When someone apologizes for their error, it ensures you that they are aware of it, and it relieves you of the uncomfortable job of having to inform them of it. But even more, when someone is truly sorry, you don't want them to feel sorry. You want to cheer them up, because they're already feeling the weight of their mistakes.

Defensive people rarely get to see the power in this, as they are too busy working on their excuses, going to great lengths to prove themselves right. How much time could be spared by instead simply apologizing? Because the truth is, while you may cling to those areas where you were right, you're not actually benefiting anyone by denying the areas where you were wrong. And if you're like most people... well then, bub... sometimes you're wrong, and you just need to admit it.

If someone finds a fault in the way you did something, rather than point to the ninety nine percent you feel you did right, simply apologize for the one percent they are noticing. All you have to lose is a little bit of pride. And in the end, most good-hearted people will come around to seeing the ninety-nine percent you did right. You free them up to do that by choosing not to defend your contributions. Once they see your wall coming down, they'll have a clearer view of all that you did right. You won't even have to show them. This is a far more powerful approach.

Recap:

To stay defensive forever, find good excuses for all that you do wrong. Get really good at proving yourself right. Whatever you do, don't apologize. Why should you? Cling to the portion you've done right, and eventually, the world will humble itself to your way of thinking. If this doesn't work the first time, argue and argue again, until everyone is too tired to keep arguing with you.

RULE # 10. NEVER TAKE ANY CRAP FROM ANYONE.

One problem with defensiveness is that we often see it as a strength. Or, better put, we feel weak for not giving into it... like we're letting others bully us around. Since we don't want to be weak, we can't let them have the last word. We won't let them win an argument feel that they've gotten the edge.

To simply allow such behavior feels oppressive... like we're letting others imprison us to their wills, taking our choices away. But what if we aren't being weak by not pushing back? What if it can actually be a choice that demonstrates great power in us, not to give into others' lower forms of communicating and acting?

In the story of the Passion, Jesus stands before Pontius Pilate. As the story goes, Pilate is trying to determine the fate of Jesus. He seems to wonder why Jesus isn't fighting back. If he had power, wouldn't he fight for his own justice?

But Jesus knows He isn't in custody because He has to be. He's there because He's chosen to be, partially to show the world a type of love it's never seen. But also, to demonstrate the invalidity of the charges being made against Him. His choice was not one of weakness, but of great strength.

In the 1940s, Gandhi led a revolution in India. His technique was similar… to fight for India's independence in a nonviolent way. His strategy was strange, yet simple. When he and his followers would get hit or knocked down, they would stand their ground, yet do so without fighting. They would stand peacefully, sometimes even being beaten or killed. Were they being pushovers? Not at all.

Their nonviolent approach propelled a strong movement that revolutionized India, and which still continues to revolutionize the way average people think and campaign for causes today. One might say that the approach Gandhi used was far more powerful than the eye-for-an-eye mentality that it contrasted, which as he said, would "leave the whole world blind."

Maybe you and I too can realize this. When we feel we are being treated unfairly by our spouses or our coworkers, or when we're frustrated by the other drivers on the road, rather than reciprocate their unfairness towards us, we can choose to love and accept them, despite their imperfect ways of acting toward us.

I don't mean we should get into the habit of tolerating physical or emotional abuse. That is simply unjustifiable, and real professional help should be sought if you or someone you know is experiencing it. What I'm talking about is the principle that in general, there is a better way to respond to others than by returning their unfairnesses. Just because someone stops giving their respect, it doesn't mean you have to stop being respectable.

One thing about life is that it simply isn't fair. No matter how loved we are, we'll still never be fully understood. Nor will we always feel valued and respected the way we want to be, or the way we feel we deserve.

Until everyone is perfect, this is just how it will be. When we feel criticized, rather than fearing that we're allowing someone else to control us, realize that we are in control. And, that we can do something far greater than argue, deflect or retaliate. We can be graceful, without their attack changing our response.

Criticism will never feel good. It might always compel us to react defensively. And, almost every worthwhile endeavor in life involves it. Whether your goal is to become a firefighter, a cop, a soldier, or to simply be a good husband, you must start out as a newbie and work your way towards becoming a pro.

EPILOGUE.

So, I hope you have acquired a few new tools to help keep you defensive forever. You now know that you should take all matters personally, even when they aren't. Realize that others' looks, tones and glances are all aimed at you.

And, make all matters into matters of worthiness. See every criticism of you as a direct assessment of your personal value. Remember that you're only as valuable as your top performance. If you start to feel unworthy, just go out and do impressive things to gain affirmation from others.

Also, never be open about your insecurities. Don't ever let others think that you trust them. You don't want to be portrayed as weak. Try not to let people help you, and of course, always trust your suspicions. This will keep you from considering that better possibilities may be likely.

Nurture your prejudices and misconceptions. Keep believing that others mean you harm (and of course, that they wish to deplete your self-worth). Expect them to be offensive before giving them a chance.

Deflect criticism. Return it to the sender. See your defensiveness as other people's problem, justified by their immaturity and unfairness. Do whatever you must in order to make your points loud and clear. Win every argument at the expense of your relationships.

Do not be aware of how destructive your defensive actions are. Do not notice when your inner thermometer is rising. There's no point in trying to deescalate the situation.

Do not re-center your focus on what matters and do not be concerned with results. Give your attention and energy, not to the message, but to the way it is being delivered. Be sure not to apologize, even if your mistake was small. Instead, redirect everyone's eyes back to all that you do right. Stand your

ground even when nobody's trying to take it. And of course,

don't take any crap from anyone.

THE END

Dear reader,

If you have any questions, comments or concerns, feel free to email me at Newbooksforyou@Hotmail.com. Please mention if you'd like to be on the mailing list too, so that you'll stay updated with free book offers as new books are released. If you'd like to see which other books and products I have to offer, please visit www.Authorcaleb.com.

Please take a moment to review this book. Remember that writers need help in order to stay writing (and in order to stay growing). Thanks so much for your time, support and interest!

C J Kruse

OTHER BOOKS BY C J KRUSE:

10 Ways To Make Sure You Never Find Happiness:

A book about Happiness, and how (not) to find it.

To Blame A Sunset:

An introspective book about life's emptiness and how to live with it.

Practice Makes Harmony:

A very practical manual for married couples who want to restore their harmony.

The 28 Day Marriage Challenge:

A one-month Christian-based marriage calendar for couples.

Meeting Rich:

A true story about the last 3 weeks of Rich Mullins life.

Printed in Great Britain
by Amazon

82228568R00047